MW01005682

INFANT JESUS
OF PRAGUE

*"The more you honor Me, the more
I will bless you."*
—The Infant Jesus of Prague

TAN Books
Charlotte, North Carolina

NIHIL OBSTAT: William W. Baum, S.T.D.
                  Censor Librorum

IMPRIMATUR: ✝ Charles H. Helmsing
                  Bishop of Kansas City-St. Joseph
                  August 29, 1962

First TAN edition, 1975. Reprinted in 1976, 1977, 1978,
1983, 1986, 1987, 1990, etc.

ISBN: 978-0-89555-106-1

Quantity Discounts available.
Go to www.tanbooks.com
or
call us at 800-437-5876
for more information.

TAN Books
Charlotte, North Carolina
1975

Introduction

DEVOTION to the Infant Jesus of Prague is devotion to the Child Jesus. It is veneration of the Son of God, who in the form of an infant chose a stable for a palace, a manger for a cradle, and shepherds for worshippers. Our Savior grants special graces to all who venerate His sacred Infancy.

The image of the Child Jesus known as the "Infant Jesus of Prague" was in reality of Spanish origin. In the 17th century, this beautiful statue was brought by a Spanish princess to Bohemia and presented to a Carmelite monastery. For many years this statue has been enshrined on a side altar in the Church of Our Lady of Victory in the city of Prague.* It is of wax, and is about nineteen inches high. It is clothed in a royal mantle, and has a beautiful jeweled crown on its head. Its right hand is

---

* The image on the front cover of this booklet is taken from a photo of the miraculous statue.

raised in blessing; its left holds a globe signifying sovereignty.

So many graces have been received by those who invoke the Divine Child before the original statue that it has been called "The Miraculous Infant Jesus of Prague." We read the following in an old book printed in Kempt: "All who approach the miraculous statue and pray there with confidence receive assistance in danger, consolation in sorrows, aid in poverty, comfort in anxiety, light in spiritual darkness, streams of grace in dryness of soul, health in sickness, and hope in despair.

In thanksgiving for the numerous graces and cures received, the miraculous statue at Prague was solemnly crowned on the Sunday after Easter, in 1665.

What is said of the original statue may be applied also to the images of the "Little King" which are venerated the world over. From small beginnings, this devotion has grown to great proportions. The Divine Child attracts an ever-increasing number of clients who appeal to Him in every need.

Origin of the Devotion

AS PREVIOUSLY mentioned, the statue of the Infant Jesus of Prague was brought to Bohemia by a Spanish princess, whose mother had given it to her as a wedding gift. This noble lady, in turn, presented the image to her daughter. When the latter's husband died, in 1623, she resolved to spend the remainder of her days in works of piety and charity.

She was particularly generous to the Carmelites of Prague who, after Emperor Ferdinand II, their founder, had removed his residence to Vienna, fell into such utter destitution that at times they had scarcely enough to eat. Accordingly, she presented her beloved statue to the religious with these prophetic words: "I hereby give you what I prize most highly in this world. **As long as you venerate this image you will not be in want.**"

Her prediction was verified. As long as the Divine Infant was venerated, God showed Himself a kind helper, through His

Son, and the community prospered both spiritually and temporally. But when the devotion to the Infant was relaxed, God's blessing seemed to depart from the house.

The statue was set up in the oratory of the monastery, and twice a day special devotions were performed before it. Here the religious sought relief in their bitter need from Him who for love of mankind had become poor.

The novices were particularly devoted to the Holy Infant. One of them, Cyrillus a Matre Dei, who was most devoted to the Holy Infant, found sudden relief from interior trials through this devotion.

Forgotten

However, the devotion to the Divine Infant was short-lived. On account of the disturbances of the Thirty Years' War, the novitiate was removed to Munich, Germany, in 1630. With Brother Cyrillus and the other novices, the most fervent worshippers of the Infant of Prague had departed. The special devotions held before the image were gradually neglected. The prosperity of the community declined, and need and distress were again felt.

Then, King Gustavus Adolphus of Sweden, the inveterate foe of Catholicism, invaded Germany. Many inhabitants fled from Prague, among them all but two of the members of the Carmelite monastery.

On November 15, 1631, the enemy took possession of the churches of the city. The Carmelite monastery was plundered, and the image of the Infant of Prague was thrown upon a heap of rubbish behind the high altar. Both hands were broken off by the fall, but, though made of wax, it was otherwise undamaged. Here the Miraculous Infant lay for seven years, forgotten by all. During this period the monastery suffered many reverses.

Found

On the feast of Pentecost, 1637, Father Cyrillus a Matre Dei, the very one who, while a novice, had been delivered from a most annoying dryness of soul through his fervent devotion to the Holy Infant, returned to Prague. Unfortunately, Prague was again overrun by hostile armies. The distress was indescribable. In this extremity the prior assembled the community to offer humble prayers to appease God's wrath.

Father Cyrillus now remembered the favors formerly received through the Infant of Prague, and with the prior's consent searched the monastery, until he found the long-lost treasure, almost buried in dust. Full of joy and gratitude, he kissed the disfigured statue and then placed it on an altar in the oratory. The long-forgotten devotions were now revived with renewed vigor. The religious disclosed their needs to the Divine Infant, and with Him they found strength and consolation.

Veneration Revived

As in former years, Father Cyrillus was the most zealous disciple of the Holy Infant. One day, when praying before the statue, he distinctly heard these words: **Have pity on Me, and I will have pity on you. Give Me My hands, and I will give you peace. The more you honor Me, the more I will bless you.**

Father Cyrillus was awestruck at these words, for he had not noticed that the hands of the Divine Infant were missing, owing to the mantle in which the figure was clad. Hastening to the prior he begged him to have the image repaired. But the prior considered the community too poor to incur this seemingly needless expense.

Then Father Cyrillus, through the Blessed Virgin, begged the Heavenly Father to send sufficient alms to have the statue repaired. His confidence was rewarded. Three days later, he was called to the sickbed of a wealthy man, to whom he related the history of the remarkable statue. The sick man at once gave a generous sum of money for the purpose of having it repaired. The prior, however, decided to buy an entirely new statue. But the Divine Infant soon manifested His displeasure. Scarcely had the new statue been put in place when it was shattered by a falling candlestick. The old and mutilated image was destined to continue as an object of veneration in the monastery.

The prior's successor, Father Dominic of St. Nicholas, owing to lack of funds found it impossible to fulfill the wish of Father Cyrillus. Again the disappointed Father Cyrillus, through the Mother of God, begged the Divine Infant to send his superiors the necessary funds to repair the image.

One day a woman gave him a large sum of money. When he wished to thank her, she had disappeared; no one had seen her come or go. The happy friar then knelt before the altar of Our Lady of the Scapular and offered gratitude to heaven.

The prior, however, assigned to him only a very small part of the sum for the repairing of the statue. This proved to be insufficient, and Father Cyrillus found himself as far as ever from attaining his object. Once more he took his troubles to the Divine Infant. On this occasion he heard these words: "Place Me near the entrance of the sacristy and you will receive aid." He did so and returned to his room, filled with hope, recommending all to his Heavenly Mother. Soon a stranger came to the sacristy, who offered to have the image repaired at his own expense. The prior accepted his offer and in a few days the repaired statue was exposed for veneration in the church. The Infant richly repaid the stranger for this good deed.

Meanwhile, new afflictions visited the community. A pestilence broke out in the city. The prior, too, became dangerously ill. When his attention was called to the Divine Infant, he vowed to say Holy Mass before the image for nine successive days, if he recovered. At once he felt relief and in a few days was completely restored to health.

He fulfilled the vow and from that time forward fervently promoted veneration of the Miraculous Infant.

Some time later there again was great need in the monastery. The prior then led prayers to the Divine Infant, in which all the members of the community took part. After three days, a generous donation was given to them unexpectedly. The statue of the holy Infant was then removed to the church so that the people could also venerate the miraculous image.

In 1641, a woman donated a large sum of money to the monastery, expressing the desire that an altar be erected to the Most Holy Trinity. This was done, and the miraculous image was placed in a magnificent gold-plated shrine for public veneration.

In 1642, a noble woman had a chapel built for the Divine Infant. This chapel was dedicated on the feast of the Holy Name in 1644, and Mass was then celebrated in

it for the first time. The feast of the Holy Name of Jesus thus became the principal feast of the Miraculous Infant of Prague.

Devotion to the Holy Infant has continued to spread throughout the world. Favors are continually reported.

The Saints and the Infant Jesus

Devotion to the Infant Jesus of Prague is, as was said, devotion to the Child Jesus, to the Son of God who became man for our salvation. This devotion was particularly popular in the Middle Ages with great saints like Bernard of Citeaux and Francis of Assisi. Their own tender love for the humanity of Our Lord found outlet in hymns, poems, songs and sermons that attracted others to this devotion.

Closer to our own day, St. Therese of Lisieux had a great love for the Infant Savior. She is known as Saint Therese of the Child Jesus, the name she took at her religious profession. A statue of the Infant was her special charge in the Carmel. Her "little way" is based on the simplicity and trust of a child in our relationship with God. Among the prayers she composed is this one: "O eternal Father, Your only Son, the dear Child Jesus, is mine, since You have given Him to me. I offer You the infinite merits of His divine childhood, and I beg You in His name to open the gates of Heaven to a countless host of little ones who will forever follow this divine Lamb."

Meaning of this Devotion

That canonized saints and so many others have recognized the need of devotion to the Infant King is not hard to understand. Far back in Old Testament times the prophet Isaias spoke of a little "shoot" that was to bud from the stock of Jesse (*Is.* 11). The spirit of the Lord would rest on this one of David's line and at His coming there would be messianic peace throughout the land, for "a little child shall lead them." The evangelists of the New Testament see this prophecy fulfilled in Christ. He is the true Prince of Peace so long awaited. Son of Mary, who is of David's line, He is at the same time the eternal Son of God.

God has placed in men's hearts an instinctive response to the helplessness of childhood. It is His Will that this response, as all others, be made to His Son, who "being rich, became poor for your sake, in order that by His poverty you might become rich." (*2 Cor.* 8:9). God ordained that Jesus should know all life's stages: infancy, childhood, youth, that He should be like us in everything, except sin. Our Lord knew the frailty of babyhood. He had to be nursed and carried about in Mary's arms, to watch with wondering eyes the world unfolding to His growing intelligence. There is no stage of growth that Jesus has not sanctified for us by living it Himself. And childhood seems to hold a special place in His heart. For as a grown man, it was a child whom He took in His arms to hold up as a model for His disciples. "Who is the greatest in the kingdom of heaven?" they had asked Him. Christ's answer was: I tell you, unless you change and become like children, you will never get into the kingdom of heaven at all! Anyone, therefore, who is as unassuming as this child is the greatest in the kingdom of heaven. (*Matt.* 18:1-5).

This teaching should not be misunderstood. Jesus is not commending childishness, timidity, lack of spiritual maturity. The Infant of Prague is pictured wearing a crown, with a globe in one small hand, and this is not without meaning. "The government is on His shoulder," we sing in the Introit of the third Mass for Christmas Day. The Child of Bethlehem was born with a mission of salvation. Being a follower of Christ demands courage, decisive action, maturity. But coupled with these must always be humility, candor, confidence— those virtues of childhood. It is these virtues that Jesus is recommending. A child accepts himself for what he is. Undismayed by falls and setbacks, he gets up again and begins over. A child is confident: he trusts his parents, believes what they tell him and asks simply for what he needs. And a child is honest; his forthright candor and simplicity in dealing with others can help us to see what our relationship with God and our neighbor should be.

Our Lord often called His followers "little ones." They were His "little flock" to whom the Father gave the kingdom. (*Luke* 12:32). This is a title of humility and love, a title suited to the Master who used it, for He is "meek and humble of heart." Devotion to the Christ Child is a means of appreciating this humility and love, a means of having in us the mind of Christ Jesus, as St. Paul urges. (*Phil.* 2:5).

The Child of Bethlehem was born to die

for us, to make us children of God; "to as many as received Him He gave the power of becoming sons of God." (*John* 1:12). Devotion to Him impresses its own special character on our piety, blending the joy of adoration with a sense of intimacy. This Child is the omnipotent God, yet He is also man in all the frailness of our flesh. He is the immortal God, yet as man He will die for us. The whole of creation is modeled on Him who is the image of the Father, yet He is born on earth and grows up in small Palestinian villages, little local towns of no fame. His Father in Heaven is the eternal God, yet His father on earth was a carpenter, a man who worked with his hands and taught his Son to do the same. These contrasts of majesty and humility, of power and weakness, give harmony and depth to the tenderness of our devotion to Christ in His childhood, mingling in our hearts a trusting and affectionate love with total adoration.

Through the Child to the Father

Devotion such as this to Our Lord's infancy leads us to His Father. Christ came to earth to lead us back to this Father in Heaven. There was always the loving reverence of a child for his father in Our Lord. He spoke of Him with filial pride and gravitated toward Him throughout His life. When Mary and Joseph found Him in the temple after their anxious search, the boy Christ answered their worried question with the simple: "Did you not realize that I must be about My Father's business?" His last words on the Cross were those of surrender to Him: "Father, into Your hands I commend My spirit." His Father's Will was food and drink to Christ: "My food is doing the will of Him who sent Me and finishing His work." (*John* 4:34). Always He showed utter confidence in His Father: "Father, I know that You always hear Me." (*John* 11:42). It was His mission to reveal God the Father's merciful, steadfast love for us, His estranged children, to reclaim us for Him.

Hand-in-hand with Christ we, too, "go to the Father." (*John* 16:28). Love for our Infant Saviour teaches us to accept—as He did—our littleness, our poverty as creatures. It teaches us, as St. Paul was taught, that "My grace is sufficient for you, for power is made perfect in infirmity." (*2 Cor.* 12:9). This devotion shows us that God's power is attracted by our very weakness, for when dealing with our human frailty, God's power is mercy. The proud and arrogant, God scatters. "He has put down the mighty from their thrones," as Our Lady sang in her *Magnificat*. But the little and humble He loves. "He has exalted the lowly." (*Lk.* 1:52).

This devotion to the Christ Child also teaches us a daring confidence in our heavenly Father. He shows His power most of all, as the Collect prayer for the 10th Sunday after Pentecost reminds us, by pardoning and granting mercy. It is from His Son that we learn how much our Father yearns to show us His love and hear our prayers. "If one of you asks his father for a loaf, will he hand him a stone, or for a fish, will he hand him a serpent, or if he asks for an egg, will he hand him a scorpion? Therefore, if you, evil as you are, know how to give good gifts to your children, how much more will your heavenly Father give . . ." (*Luke* 11:11–13).

God created us in order to have those to whom He could give. We praise our Father by receiving His gifts. Our Lord told us of the great joy of finding a lost sheep. God's joy in us is the joy of a saviour. We cannot give Him anything He does not already have. He receives something only when we accept His gifts. The joy of our Father in Heaven, then, is the same joy of a father on earth when his child asks his aid lovingly and confidently. When our prayer comes to Him through Christ, His beloved Son, He will not fail to hear it, for "in this is the love, not that we have loved God, but that He has first loved us and sent His Son a propitiation for our sins." (*1 John* 4:10).

Prayers to the Holy Infant Jesus

Offering of Mass in His Honor

*The following prayers may be
said before Mass, or any other time.*

O DIVINE CHILD JESUS! As You called the shepherds to Your crib by Your holy angels, and the wise men by a wonderful star, so You called me today to the adoration of Your Divinity and Humanity, to the holy Sacrifice of the Mass.

The three holy kings offered gold, incense and myrrh; I, however, offer You to Your Heavenly Father (for You are mine), through the hands of the priest, just as You offered Yourself to Him lying in the crib, a poor helpless Child.

I unite my intention with the intention of the priest and the whole Catholic Church, and will assist at this Holy Mass with the greatest devotion, to Your honor, in memory of Your bitter sufferings which began in the stable of Bethlehem. I offer it in thanksgiving for all the good I have received, as atonement for my many sins and negligences, and finally to obtain Your assistance, most gracious Infant, in my necessities, especially in this need. . . . (*Here mention your intention.*)

I unite this Sacrifice with the bloody sacrifice which You, O Jesus, offered on the Cross. I offer it for myself, for all my relatives, friends and benefactors, living and dead, for the spiritual and civil authorities and for all mankind.

Graciously accept this Sacrifice, O most kind Father and Lord, and hear my prayers through Your beloved Son, who became a little child and let Himself be laid in the crib.

O almighty and eternal God, our Creator and Redeemer, graciously regard our prayers and accept with a favorable and benign countenance the Sacrifice of the saving Victim which we are about to offer to Your Majesty in honor of Your Son, our Lord Jesus Christ: that through the pouring forth of Your grace upon us we may rejoice that our names are written in Heaven under the glorious Name of Jesus, as a pledge of eternal predestination.

Through the same Christ our Lord. Amen.

Prayer of
Rev. Cyrillus a Matre Dei

*The first and most devoted venerator of the
Miraculous Infant Jesus of Prague*

JESUS, unto Thee I flee,
Through Thy Mother praying Thee
In my need to succor me.
Truly, I believe of Thee
God Thou art with strength to shield me;
Full of trust, I hope of Thee
Thou Thy grace wilt give to me.
All my heart I give to Thee,
Therefore, do my sins repent me;
From them breaking, I beseech Thee,
Jesus, from their bonds to free me.
Firm my purpose is to mend me;
Never more will I offend Thee.
Wholly unto Thee I give me,
Patiently to suffer for Thee,
Thee to serve eternally.
And my neighbor like to me
I will love for love of Thee.
Little Jesus, I beseech Thee,
In my need to succor me,
That with Joseph and Mary
And the Angels, I may Thee
Once enjoy eternally. Amen.

Novena Prayer

Asterisks are inserted to mark pauses
when prayed by a group of persons.

O DEAREST JESUS, tenderly loving us, * Your greatest joy is to dwell among us and to bestow Your blessing upon us! * Though I am not worthy that You should behold me with love, * I feel myself drawn to You, O dear Infant Jesus, * because You gladly pardon me and exercise Your almighty power over me.

So many who turned with confidence to You * have received graces and had their petitions granted. * Behold me, in spirit I kneel before Your miraculous image on Your altar in Prague, * and lay open my heart to You, * with its prayers, petitions and hopes. * Especially the affair of . . . I enclose in Your loving Heart. * Govern me and do with me and mine according to Your holy Will, * for I know that in Your Divine wisdom and love You will ordain everything for the best. * Almighty gracious Infant Jesus, do not withdraw Your hand from us, * but protect and bless us forever.

I pray You, sweetest Infant, * in the name of Your Blessed Mother Mary who cared for You with such tenderness, * and by the great reverence with which St. Joseph carried You in his arms, * comfort me and make me happy * that I may bless and thank You forever from all my heart. Amen.

Litany of the Miraculous Infant
For private devotion only.

Lord, have mercy. *Christ, have mercy.*
Lord, have mercy. Christ, hear us. *Christ, graciously hear us.*
God, the Father of heaven, *have mercy on us.*
God the Son, Redeemer of the world, *have mercy on us.*
God the Holy Spirit, *etc.*

O miraculous Infant Jesus,
Infant Jesus, true God and Lord,
Infant Jesus, whose omnipotence is manifested in a wonderful manner,
Infant Jesus, whose wisdom searches our hearts and minds,
Infant Jesus, whose goodness continually inclines to aid us,
Infant Jesus, whose providence leads us to our last end and destiny,
Infant Jesus, whose truth enlightens the darkness of our hearts,
Infant Jesus, whose generosity enriches our poverty,

Infant Jesus, whose friendship consoles
the afflicted,

Infant Jesus, whose mercy forgives our
sins,

Infant Jesus, whose strength invigorates us,

Infant Jesus, whose power turns away
all evils,

Infant Jesus, whose justice deters us
from sin,

Infant Jesus, whose power conquers Hell,

Infant Jesus, whose lovely countenance
attracts our hearts,

Infant Jesus, whose greatness holds the
universe in its hand,

Infant Jesus, whose love-inflamed Heart
kindles our cold hearts,

Infant Jesus, whose miraculous hand raised
in benediction fills us with all blessings,

Infant Jesus, whose sweet and holy Name
rejoices the hearts of the faithful,

Infant Jesus, whose glory fills the whole
world,

Be merciful. *Spare us, O Jesus.*
Be merciful. *Graciously hear us, O Jesus.*

From all evil, *Deliver us, O Jesus.*
From all sin, *Deliver us, O Jesus.*
From all distrust of Your infinite
goodness, *etc.*

From all doubts in Your power of miracles,
From all lukewarmness in Your veneration,
From all trials and misfortunes,
Through the mysteries of Your holy
   childhood,

We sinners beseech You, *hear us.*
Through the intercession of Mary,
   Your Virgin Mother, and St. Joseph,
   Your foster father, *We beseech You,
   hear us.*
That You would pardon us, *We beseech You,
   hear us.*
That You would bring us to true
   repentance, *etc.*
That You would preserve and increase
   in us love and devotion to Your
   sacred infancy,
That You would never withdraw Your
   miraculous hand from us,
That You would keep us mindful of
   Your numberless benefits,
That You would inflame us more and more
   with love for Your Sacred Heart,
That You would graciously hear all who
   call upon You with confidence,
That You would preserve our country
   in peace,
That You would free us from all
   impending evils,

That You would give eternal life to all
who act generously toward You,

That You would pronounce a merciful
sentence on us at the judgment,

That You would in Your miraculous image
remain our consoling refuge,

Jesus, Son of God and of Mary,

Lamb of God, who take away the sins
of the world, *Spare us, O Jesus.*

Lamb of God, who take away the sins of
the world, *Graciously hear us, O Jesus.*

Lamb of God, who take away the sins of
the world, *Have mercy on us.*

Jesus, hear us.
Jesus, graciously hear us.

Our Father, etc.

Let Us Pray

O Miraculous Infant Jesus, prostrate
before Your sacred image, we beseech You
to cast a merciful look on our troubled
hearts. Let Your tender Heart, so inclined
to pity, be softened at our prayers, and
grant us that grace for which we ardently
implore You. Take from us all affliction and
despair, all trials and misfortunes with
which we are laden. For Your sacred
Infancy's sake hear our prayers and send

us consolation and aid, that we may praise You, with the Father and the Holy Spirit, forever and ever. Amen.

Prayer To Be Said by a Sick Person

(May be used for a novena)

O MERCIFUL INFANT JESUS! I know of Your miraculous deeds for the sick. How many diseases You cured during Your blessed life on earth, and how many venerators of Your miraculous image ascribe to You their recovery and deliverance from most painful and hopeless maladies. I know, indeed, that a sinner like me has merited his sufferings and has no right to ask for favors. But in view of the innumerable graces and the miraculous cures granted even to the greatest sinners through the veneration of Your holy infancy, particularly in the miraculous statue of Prague or in representations of it, I exclaim with the greatest assurance: O most loving, most pitiful Infant Jesus, You can cure me if You will! Do not hesitate, O Heavenly Physician, if it be Your Will that I recover from this present illness; extend Your most holy hands, and by Your power take away all pain and infirmity, so that my recovery may be due, not to natural remedies, but to You alone. If, however, You in Your inscrutable wisdom have determined otherwise, then at least restore my soul to perfect health, fill me with heavenly consolation and blessing, that I may be like You, O Jesus, in my sufferings, and may glorify Your providence until You, at the death of my body, bestow on me eternal life. Amen.

Novena for the Nine Days Preceding the 25th of Each Month

1. Eternal Father, I offer to Your honor and glory, for my eternal salvation and for the salvation of the whole world, the mystery of the birth of our Divine Redeemer. *Glory be, etc.*

2. Eternal Father, I offer to Your honor and glory, and for my eternal salvation and that of the whole world, the sufferings of the most holy Virgin and St. Joseph on that long and weary journey from Nazareth to Bethlehem, and the anguish of their hearts at not finding a place of shelter when the Saviour of the world was about to be born. *Glory be, etc.*

3. Eternal Father, I offer to Your honor and glory, and for my eternal salvation and that of the whole world, the sufferings of Jesus in the manger where He was born, the cold He suffered, the tears He shed and His tender infant cries. *Glory be, etc.*

4. Eternal Father, I offer to Your honor and glory, and for my eternal salvation and that of the whole world, the pain which the Divine Child Jesus felt in His tender Body when He submitted to the rite of circumcision: I offer You that Precious Blood which He then first shed for the salvation of all mankind. *Glory be, etc.*

5. Eternal Father, I offer to Your honor and glory, and for my eternal salvation and that of the whole world, the humility, mortification, patience, charity and all the virtues of the Child Jesus; I thank You, I love You, and I bless You tenderly for this ineffable mystery of the Incarnation of the Word of God. *Glory be, etc.*

V. The Word was made Flesh,

R. And dwelt among us.

LET US PRAY

O God, whose only-begotten Son has appeared in the substance of our flesh; grant, we beg You, that through Him, whom we acknowledge to have been outwardly like us, we may deserve to be renewed in our inward selves. Who lives and reigns with You for ever and ever. Amen.

Powerful Novena in Urgent Need

(In cases of great urgency, a novena of hours may be made instead of days. The prayers should, if possible, be repeated at the same time every hour for nine consecutive hours.)

O JESUS, who said, "Ask and you shall receive, seek and you shall find, knock and it shall be opened to you," through the intercession of Mary, Your most holy Mother, I knock, I seek, I ask that my prayer be granted. (*Mention your request.*)

O JESUS, who said, "All that you ask of the Father in My Name He will grant you," through the intercession of Mary, Your most holy Mother, I humbly and urgently ask Your Father in Your Name that my prayer be granted. (*Mention your request.*)

O JESUS, who said, "Heaven and earth shall pass away, but My word shall not pass," through the intercession of Mary, Your most holy Mother, I feel confident that my prayer will be granted. (*Mention your request.*)

Prayer of Thanksgiving For Graces Received from The Infant Jesus

I PROSTRATE MYSELF before Your holy image, O most gracious Infant Jesus, to offer You my most fervent thanks for the blessings You have bestowed on me. I shall incessantly praise Your ineffable mercy and confess that You alone are my God, my helper, and my protector. Henceforth my entire confidence shall be placed in You! Everywhere I will proclaim aloud Your mercy and generosity, so that Your great love and the great deeds which You perform through this miraculous image may be acknowledged by all. May devotion to Your holy infancy increase more and more in the hearts of all Christians, and may all who experience Your assistance persevere with me in showing unceasing gratitude to Your most holy infancy, to which be praise and glory forever. Amen.